HORSE: A PORTRAIT

HORSE: A PORTRAIT

A Photographer's Life With Horses

CHRISTIANE SLAWIK

WILLOW CREEK PRESS

Translated from the original German text by Susanne Schruefer

Published by Willow Creek Press
P.O. Box 147, Minocqua, Wisconsin 54548

Editor: Andrea Donner

Library of Congress Cataloging-in-Publication Data:

Slawik, Christiane, 1964-
    Horse : a portrait : a photographer's life with horses / Christiane Slawik.
        p. cm.
    Includes bibliographical references and index.
    ISBN 978-1-59543-596-5 (hardcover : alk. paper)
  1. Photography of horses. 2. Horses–Pictorial works. 3. Slawik, Christiane, 1964-
I. Title
    TR729.H6S63 2007
    779'.3296655–dc22

                                                2007003150

Printed in Italy

Preface

All my life I have been fascinated by horses in a way that I can hardly put into words. Instead, I try to capture this feeling with my camera—this one special, magical moment that I can take home in my heart and that I can share with others through my photos.

This moment can be everything: power and elegance, vitality combined with a wild and at the same time gentle spirit. Beauty, innocence and curiosity, and the ever-lasting, incredible will to please mankind.

Horses should not merely be regarded as useful animals: They are so much more.

These wonderful creatures are our partners—infinitely patient, attentive, and always ready to give their all. They make us proud; they give us the gift of happiness, harmony, and inner peace. They make our souls smile.

If only we allow them, they even help us to form our characters and make us rise above ourselves.

Horses are the most amazing creatures I know. Thank you for the many unfor-gettable hours that I have had the opportunity to spend in your company!

Christiane Slawik

Contents

Show Time!

They are the "icing on the cake"—striking four-legged personalities—horses and ponies seeping with charisma. A look, a swish of the tail, a snort is enough and you are under their spell—be it a stallion, a mare, or a foal. At first sight they may seem inconspicuous, but once they move or are ridden they unfold their true self like a butterfly. Others are eye-catchers right from the start in their proportions, their color, or their type, and they seem to know how beautiful they truly are. Why are these animals so different, so fascinating, and so irresistible? Why can I never get enough of them; why can't I stop photographing them? Are humans especially attached to them, so overwhelmingly self-confident and effervescent with vitality? Or is it only me who personifies them?

Photo shoots with such horses are always a special treat. Sometimes I have the feeling that we are kindred spirits, that they are only performing for me to admire them. Telepathically, I know that they will gallop three strides more before they come to a halt and gaze directly into my camera with a look saying: "Wasn't that wonderful? Did you get a good photo?"

Desperado Malbec was one the first of those memorable creatures that I met. My first sight of him was a photo in a cheap calendar that I put on my desk. Even in this unspectacular pose, this chestnut "no-name" horse radiated so much pertness, self-confidence, and charm that I kept the photo glued to my ring binder all through my college studies. Years later, when we worked on a western riding documentary, our paths crossed again. When the stallions were presented I had déjà vu: my long standing

A perfect model, Desperado Malbec seemed to jump on cue for me.

Opposite: Although in their twenties, these old horses could still strut their stuff for the camera.

dream horse was right in front of me in flesh and blood! I could not believe my eyes. European champion Desperado was no longer a spring chicken, yet he twinkled at me as cocky and adventurous as in the picture on my ring binder. In the round pen he romped around like a clown, bursting with energy—just as I had always imagined him.

Only once was I able to photograph him. I had a vision of the photograph in my mind and amazingly, Desperado bucked into the air exactly on the spot I had imagined. The stallion jerked to a halt and turned to look at me questioningly: "Any problems?" He made a showy gesture with his head, started to gallop and did the same stunt on the same spot before stopping again: "Hope you got it this time—Now you knew what would happen!" To be on the safe side, the Quarter Horse did it a third time and then made his exit in a cloud of dust. It turned out that I had taken the same, spectacular photo three times. It became a cover picture and many people asked me if we had retouched the jump the horse took. The photo is very old and does not meet the quality standards that I have today, but it is still one of my favorites. Never again have I witnessed such behavior. Desperado Malbec was exceptional in every way.

Oldies but Goodies crossed my way in southern Germany in early summer 2006. Some good-humored ladies decided to have me immortalize their aged seniors. Very early in the morning, the gang of retirees—turned out to their best—was ready to start. During the last few years, leisurely hacks and quiet walks in the countryside had kept the oldies, well advanced in their twenties, from becoming too rusty. Yet, on this day everything was different, as the seniors Americh, Walido, Bluepoint and Co. noticed immediately: extensive grooming, bandages on the legs, manes braided, new saddle pads… Goody! Now we are important again, they seemed to feel. Alertly, the former competition horses watched our every move with pricked ears, flared nostrils and eyes shining in delight. It was obvious that they enjoyed being in the limelight and they kept this up throughout the photo shoot. As soon as one of the geldings did his solo performance in front of the camera, the others seemed to push to the front to be the next in the "show ring." Running free, they all behaved like three-year-olds. They frolicked around, their feet hardly touching the ground and were eager to present themselves at their very best. We had loads of fun together and in the end nobody could quite believe that the horses portrayed on the photos were altogether more than one hundred years old.

Charismatic horses can often be found among the showing breeds. Whenever they are in front of a camera they shine at their best. However, I have never seen them in any other situation nor have I watched them out at pasture, so I do not know how they behave if they are totally free. Denmark's Golden Playboy was well known in the Saddlebred scene. He made his first appearance in Europe under Lisa Rosenberger. Down-to-earth Germany did not have an altogether unambiguous attitude towards the palomino horse with the long tail. Dark bay warmbloods without markings—not "Barbie horses"—are more the preferred type in these regions. Yet, when the ostensible "toy horse" showed off in rack under his world-class rider, the audience was drawn in by the horse's charisma and his spectacular movements. As long as he was in the arena, even the most conservative of riders could not keep their eyes off the Saddlebred—of course, they would not admit it in public. I have loved Golden Boy from the moment I first saw him, a showman body and soul. He had a way of turning his fine neck and head toward my camera that made me feel as if I had just been received in an audience.

Josef's Walkaway Farm is the biggest stud farm for Tennessee Walking Horses in Europe. Its stallions are not only extremely beautiful, but they also have such sound characters that there is no risk in letting a beginner hack out with them. I would even entrust them with my non-riding husband (and that says a lot!). Oles Blue Sawdust, Labeled in Gold, Prides Gold Gypsy Boy, and the others had a hell of a good time playing with me in their pasture. They galloped and racked flat out and simply couldn't get enough. The grooms did not have quite as much fun getting all the horses ready for the photo shoot! In the end, however, they all agreed that the photos were worth the hard labor. At this point, a huge thank you to all the grooms around the world—without you we photographers would be lost!

Above and overleaf: The beautiful Tennessee Walking Horses of Josef's Walkaway Farm.

Opposite: Golden Playboy

Seasonal Bliss:
Variety Guaranteed

In regards to photography, weather conditions in Central, Western, and Northern Europe are rarely ideal. Only once in a great while does the weather grant you perfect lighting conditions. Thinking of my colleagues in Florida and California, I am green with envy, yet… I have something different to boast of: a life full of excitement. Will I have to reschedule the photo shoot at the stud farm five times due to extensive weather lows or will it, for once, work out the first time? Will I have at least a few seconds to photograph the spotlessly clean, white stallion before he turns into an Appaloosa or some other kind of spotted horse after galloping a couple of strides in the muddy field? Will I spend a whole week, or maybe only three days, twiddling my thumbs in Northern Germany or Ireland, waiting for the pouring rain to subside?

There is some consolation for the damp nuisances: you appreciate the sun a lot more when he smiles radiantly from blue skies all day. In our part of the world, nature celebrates the change of seasons with so much more splendor than in the sun-blessed regions of the world, and I relish it to the fullest! Every few months, themes and motifs vary—it is never boring!

There are enchanting moments in spring with its soft light and tender green, with the first foals starting to discover their world, walking inquisitively through flowery meadows on shaky legs. It is breathtaking in summer to watch a herd of horses gallop into the sunset after a hot summer day. Bright autumn colors are eye-catching and make showy backgrounds, while the energy and power of a stallion plowing his way through deep snow on a clear, bright winter day is nothing short of fascinating.

Classical Baroque Dressage

Riding as an Art

When I photograph horses under the saddle, my main purpose is to capture the harmony between horse and rider. Often I find this harmony with riders who adhere to the Baroque riding tradition. Without any ambition of winning at shows and without any time restraint, these cultured horse lovers school their horses, often of the typical Baroque type—such as Iberian, Friesian, Knabstrup, Lipizzaner, or Klabdruby horses—with such dedication, expertise, and light hands to create a four-legged ballet dancer up to haute école level. Patiently, they follow the teachings of the classical Baroque and Renaissance riding masters, for whom only the horse itself determines the duration and the course of its training. Through their perfect movements in piaffe, passage, half-pass, and the levade, they elevate riding to an art. Historical riding accessories and costumes add to the splendor of the refined riding performances of these modern masters in the saddle.

In Copenhagen, I documented the revival of the Royal Danish Riding School in the town palace of the Queen of Denmark. It was an extremely interesting week, amidst marble stables, innumerable Japanese tourists, and the omnipresent courtly protocol, which offers many opportunities to make a blunder. After the evening performance, the sun set behind the palace. There were still some fleeting sunrays in the arcades. Beside me, P.R.E. Aureolo ("the golden") walked calmly on longs reins toward the stable. I urged the rider that we had no time to lose if we still wanted to catch this fading, golden light. Silke Branderup took up the reins and quickly directed her surprised horse into the arcades.

The clomping noise of his hooves on the stone floor startled the horse. Soothingly, Silke talked to Aureolo. She only managed to pass the sun spot once before the striking setting was swallowed by the evening shadows. Yet the short sprint was worth our while: on this photo, the stallion, whose home is in Sweden, really lives up to his name!

Andrea Kahn dreamt of photos showing her black P.R.E. Dorito and herself wearing her wedding gown in an unusual environment. Due to the black-and-white contrast of the horse and dress we needed some color for the background—preferably blue. It was obvious; it had to be water. So we took horse and rider to Lake Chiemsee in Bavaria. Being a well-established team, the two of them were an overwhelming picture: the huge, powerful Dorito with his gleaming jet black coat covered in cascades of lace. The petite bride beamed with pride and joy in her ornate wedding dress. Skillfully, she asked her well-trained Andalusian stallion to dance with her on the bank of the lake. In no time at all we had several wonderful photos, but I glanced longingly at the lake: "Would you mind riding into the water?" I asked. She did, and melted with her black stallion into the deep blue, twinkling surface of the water. This picture became Andrea's dream photo, for which we paid the fair blood toll of around 400 mosquito bites!

Opposite: Andrea Kahn in the Chiemsee on P.R.E. stallion Dorito, and (left) during a September morning mist on P.R.E. stallion Dandi.

Page 28: Marisol Lopez-Candel is one of the best sidesaddle riders in the world. She bred, raised and trained her sidepassing P.R.E. stallion Nordeno all by herself. This photo shows her during the "Royal Horse Gala" in Berlin.

Page 29: The classical Portuguese horseman Carlos Pinto demonstrates a pirouette on his Lusitano stallion Notabel, which he has also been riding at the Dressage World Championships.

Friesians:

Black is Beautiful

Without a doubt, he has been galloping through your childhood dreams, as he does all around the world. A horse just like "The Black Stallion"; a horse strong, majestic, a generous heart for his human friends, his long mane blowing in the wind; full of nobility, power, and grace, giving you a gentle look with his dark eyes—you will find all this in the Friesian Horse.

It is a miracle that this breed even exists today and it only happened thanks to the passionate dedication of some true horsepeople. They succeeded in sparking off the love and enthusiasm that they themselves had felt for these horses in a large audience of people throughout the world.

The appealing black horses from Holland are highly intelligent and very eager to learn. Despite this—or maybe because of it—they are nearly always calm and easy-going. Some people would characterize them as stolid, but others cherish them as extremely trusting and honest horses with a friendly nature.

The "black pearls" set off waves of admiration and make hearts beat faster wherever they appear—sometimes unintentionally. When I let the two stallions Ludo and Janko run free in a sandpit close to a busy road, everyone thought that the steep slopes were insurmountable. Janko behaved impeccably, the perfect photo model, standing quietly like a statue. Ludo, however, being an energetic youngster, galloped around and suddenly had the "brilliant" idea of climbing one of the nearly vertical slopes. I was stunned and my heart sank into my boots. Breathing heavily, the brave Friesian nimbly worked his way up, as if it were the most natural thing in the world. Almost

at the top, he paused for a moment to look down to his friend Janko and the four humans, all of them eyeballing him anxiously. He froze. All of a sudden it seemed that his heart sank into his boots, or rather into his hooves. "Oh my God, I am all alone up here!" he neighed timidly. Janko gave him a rather indignant answer and the runaway mountaineer started to slide down the slope…. very carefully. After this adventure Ludo felt so relieved to be with us again that he was ready to do every pose we wanted—as long as he could stay on level ground!

Stallion Max is another Friesian character whom I visit from time to time in his home in rural Bavaria. Once a month, he opens his paddock or stable door and goes on his local round trip. All on his own, he trots through the valley to socialize with all kinds of fellow horses in his "circle" of close friends. In the evening he will unfailingly return, well satisfied with himself and fully informed about the latest gossip. All the horses he visits and their respective owners know this habit and nobody is alarmed by the roaming stallion. Nothing has ever happened to cause alarm… which is typical of a Friesian Horse.

Egypt:

Horses, Dust and Burning Sun

Our Taxi has been crawling through the dusty Moloch of Cairo for the last 30 minutes. Noisy traffic, a buzz of oriental voices, luxury hotels and palaces directly next to slums where children and emaciated animals are searching for something to eat in the garbage dumps; elegant residences and glorious mosques, heavily loaded donkey carts on four-lane freeways.

The hustle and bustle of Ghamal Abdel Nasser Street in Giza, right behind the pyramids, can hardly be captured in words. This street never sleeps and most of the private riding stables are located here. It's a vibrant Arabian life where the horses are its centerpiece. Horses are everywhere, hundreds of them, horses of all colors and shapes, all of them crowded into this confined space. No medium can offer you so many facets of entertainment, so many atmospheres, and such a wide variety of emotions as this somewhat run-down district on the outskirts of the metropolis. Vivacity and lethargy, pride and misery, action and thoughtfulness, joy and sorrow—you will find everything in this microcosm… Everything except boredom!

Nothing happens without Farouk Breesh; he is always around. The old man sits calmly in front of his office, a glass of tea in hand. Countless photos bear witness to the VIP's who have ridden his horses (for example, Chelsea Clinton with her mother Hilary in the background). Day in and day out, Farouk watches the busy goings-on in his neighborhood, smokes cigarettes, chats with guests, relatives, and friends, and casually makes some deal or other. All his life, he and his family have dealt with horses and worked endless hours in the stables behind the pyramids.

Already many years ago, a small number of horse dealers were located in this area. Among them was Farouk's grandfather, son of an old-established family. Then the tourists came. They wanted to explore the desert on horseback, wanted to experience the sensation of virtually flying over this vast ocean of sand on the back of a noble Arabian horse; or to go up to the pyramids, looking at them from a completely new angle—from horseback. So the natives kept up with the trend; they built larger stables and bought horses to rent them to tourists. Ten years ago there were about ten stables; today there are more than fifty. Everyone tries to make money with the horses. More than 1,000 horses have gone through Farouk's hands. He is not even sure for how long he has been in business. "I think it must be about 65 years" is his careful estimate. "Horses are in my veins. This is my home. I will never give this up." Insha Allah!

Six stables are owned by the Breesh clan with its hierarchical structure. Their name is well-known and is a guarantee for quality in Egyptian standards. Patriarch Farouk has everything under his control. With pride he shows us his favorite horses. We are surprised: No pathetic tourist horses with a sad fate, but wonderful, spirited, energetic animals, with radiant personalities are dancing for us in the sandy backyard. With a canny smile, the experienced salesman puts among them a cantankerously bleating dromedary. This incites the horses to carry their elegant necks with even more expression. The horses breeze past us, tails in the air and nostrils wide open. Apollo, the black stallion, is Farouk's crown jewel; although not a purebred and advanced in age, he is a spectacular horse. Sif, a lean but tough chestnut, belongs to Farouk's grandson. Marvelous Sanura, who competed successfully in the Dubai 75-mile endurance race, shows unbelievable gaits. In comes Ward, a dark chestnut pure-bred mare, more than twenty years old, wearing some strange ornament round her neck: an old tennis shoe. When he sees our perplexed gazes, Farouk laughs: "Even if you are not directly affected, this works really great! We use it to avert the evil eye from our very valuable horses." Oh, really!

Above: For Samy Al Bahrawy, his stallion "Prince" is more son than horse.

Opposite: The mare Sanura is a successful Distance-Racing horse and member of the Egypt National Team. With her charisma and performance, she does not need more Arabian-dish.

As soon as the gates of "El Zahraa," the National Stud farm of Egypt, are closed behind us, a completely different world opens up. In the center of this bustling city with 19 million inhabitants we have found an oasis of peace and quiet. "The flower," the translation of the Arabian name, is hidden in a side street, only 20 minutes' drive away from the airport. It is easy to overlook the plain sign pointing to the stud farm and hardly any taxi-driver even knows that it exists. Giant eucalyptus trees insulate it from the outside world and hide the neighboring high-rise buildings.

Mares and youngsters spend their days unperturbed, eating, dozing, galloping around, taking sand-baths in generous, vast sand paddocks with big, round feeding troughs, which are typical for "El Zahraa." The stallions live in spacious loose-boxes, larger than the home of many a farmer's family.

At sunrise, the horses leave their stables to spend the day outdoors. During the hot summer months, the Arabian horses are fed barley and hay; in winter fresh alfalfa, which grows on the banks of the river Nile especially for the stud farm, and is delivered daily. Each group of horses has its own team of grooms. The teams know each of "their" horses inside and out and look after them lovingly. Some of the men are third generation workers at the stud farm and are now training their sons to follow in their footsteps. When we asked the head groom which of the stallions was his favorite, he answered in the flowery oriental way: "But they are all my sons! How could I love one son more than the others?" The paddocks are kept immaculately clean and the grooms prepare their meals over an open fire behind the stables. Everything takes as long as it takes. Time passes at a different pace in the orient.

Above: There is no need for a fence in the desert. There is no place to go for the horses except to their stables with fresh water and grain. No matter if foal or stallion—they always come back!

Left: Hamed shows his Dust Dance at FB-stables in Cairo.

Opposite: Early morning at El Zahraa state stud, Cairo. The alfalfa for the precious mares is brought daily from the Nile River with donkeys and camels.

Above: Two year old asil youngster Muhab enjoys his daily turnout at FB-Stables in Cairo.

Opposite: (Top left) Harras, one of the breeding stallions at El Zahraa. (Top right) Having fun in the Red Sea at Hurghada. (Bottom) At only one and one-half years, Ramses is already a powerful young stallion!

Each of the private stud farms around Cairo is like an animated fairy tale, a well concealed paradise for four-legged treasures. In the date palm forest of Shams El Asil, Dani Barbary is offering artfully arranged tidbits from a silver tray to her graceful gems. The mares with jeweled halters daintily accept them, and then melt away among the trees like elfins. The high walls of Al Badeis conceal magnificent stables, a lush garden, and huge sand paddocks. Nasr Marei accommodates national champions as well as excellent mares with unbelievable gaits. Yet, not only Arabian Horses are the pride and joy of the Rabab Stud. If you spend enough time in the ample grounds (which are more like a botanical garden), you will find them eventually: a bunch of spotted miniature Shetland ponies! The little goblins spend their days munching all sorts of exotic plants and, being an absolute rarity in Egypt, they have the freedom to do whatever they like.

In Hurghada the setting is quite different. At the Seahorse Riding Stables, about 30 horses are waiting to carry tourists through the desert. These horses don't have papers but are perfect representatives of the classical Muniqui Arabians. Their noses are nearly straight; they are angular, tough and fast—primal purebreds through and through. For our taste, most of these horses could put on a bit of weight. But they are modest; they never eat all the chaff, barley, and pellets they are offered. Compared to the average wages, keeping horses is quite a luxury in Egypt. Walid Al Bahrawy looks well after his mares and he makes sure that not even the tiniest piece of the precious alfalfa, transported to his stables from far away Cairo, is wasted. He carefully picks up every single piece that has fallen to the ground and puts it back into the hayrack.

I am taking a good look at Dahab, whose white coat is so fine that her dark skin shines through. It is hard to believe that such a delicate horse has enough space in her narrow chest to accommodate a well-working heart and lungs. Yet, as soon as I ride her, she has convinced me: after miles of racing through desert sand, up and down dunes, Dahab shows not a sign of exhaustion, and asks for more. This unbelievable mare would never win at a show, but this gentle, wonderful, delicate horse will safely carry her rider through the desert—and that is what Arabian Horses have been bred for.

Egypt: Horses, Dust and Burning Sun 45

Unexpected Encounters

I received the call at 10 A.M. While flying over Germany in a plane, a friend of mine had spotted a large red blotch in a mountain range. A field of poppies—and only three hours' drive away from my office! Poppy fields look fantastic as a background for photographs, but they are extremely rare in this region and they wither very fast. It was now or never! Our telephone lines buzzed. In only two hours we located the owner of the field. He was on holiday in Spain, but kindly allowed us to use his field for a photo shoot. I hurriedly contacted several horse owners in the surrounding area, asked them for their support, and arranged a meeting point. At 1 P.M. we were on our way. Accidents and road blocks everywhere, but we finally reached our destination after four, sheer endless hours. A large number of all types of horses—Andalusians, Akhal-Tekhes, Arabians, Welsh Ponies, Connemara Ponies, and Norwegian Fjord Ponies—all of them spotlessly clean and beautifully turned out, were waiting for me in a long row of trailers. Some twenty minutes later, our convoy reached the poppy field, resplendent in blazing red, in the middle of nowhere. Innumerable helping hands quickly built up a fence and arranged for smooth transitions from one four-legged model to the next until the sun set at 9 P.M. At midnight we were back home with more than 1,000 new photographs. Believe me, the photographer's life is a hard one!

On another, equally stressful yet not quite so time-consuming occasion, we made a marvelous photo series in France. We were supposed to photograph Iberian stallions moving free, but instead we spent hours in the stable waiting for a raging thunderstorm to come to an end. When we had abandoned all hope for a successful photo shoot, the storm suddenly abated. The sun peered through the window. A huge, bright rainbow arched over the pastures. We could not believe our eyes and rushed hectically: someone yanked open the first stable door, grabbed the stallion, put on the halter, unraveled the braids, and headed through puddles and mud toward the pasture. Running along with them, I adjusted my camera. There was no time to lose! The light already started to fade again, the colors of the rainbow subdued. In bewilderment, Lusitano Quintal found himself standing on the lush green pasture, surrounded by fidgety humans inciting him to gallop. All of a sudden, the gray stallion exploded into a full speed gallop and, with his long mane blowing in the air, he virtually flew past the colorful wonder of nature in the last minute. Everyone was thrilled—especially the horse; although the storm resumed its rage, the horse would not allow us to catch him. In vain, we tried to lure him back into the stable. Instead, he preferred to take a lavish mud bath. That was his idea of a suitable fee for his brilliant performance.

At 11 o'clock in the morning, the Andalusian sun was already much too bright to photograph the chestnut Spanish horse. We put him in the "picadero" and made him move, constantly changing the direction. I really didn't expect the series to turn out well. Only at a second glance did I realize what a striking motif I had. The photo of the stallion spinning around toward the wall seemed unusable, but then I noticed a surprising bonus in the left hand bottom corner: the sun projected the shadow of the horse onto the wall so that it looked like an opponent was attacking and the chestnut shying away from it. Most of the time, you will need a second, wondering glance to grasp the photo, but once you have, I am sure you will appreciate its uniqueness!

In order to abstract the powerful vitality of another Andalusian stallion, I wanted to end the photo shoot with some blurred photographs of him. Therefore Hipico II had to do some final rounds at a flat out gallop. Two men vigorously pushed him forward, but the gray stallion was not amused. He seemed to think that we had taken enough photos and, visibly annoyed, violently struck out with one front leg at the very moment I released the shutter. This spontaneous "Spanish walk" made the final photo the absolute highlight of the entire series and is now the cover picture of this book.

During one of my visits to Tenerife I heard about a gorgeous Hispano-Arabian who had already won the dressage championships on the Canary Islands. Abrileno was indeed a fantastic horse, but it looked as if we could not photograph him moving free. His paddock was surrounded by all kinds of clutter, totally unsuitable as a background for photographs. Too bad. However, his owner would not allow us to leave without having duly admired his treasure, photos or no photos. He made the bay horse move back and forth and soon we could hardly see anything for all the dust. Hardly see anything? That was it! We could see neither the power supply lines nor the cars, nor the chicken coops, nor the houses, nor the tool sheds, but only Abrileno's silhouette amidst the dust kicked up by his movements. I don't mind cleaning my equipment for an hour if I get such wonderful photos….

Heavy Horses:
One Horsepower, Size Extra Extra Large

They have a quiet and docile temperament, yet they take our hearts by storm. The chubby, gentle giants evoke images and sentiments of the "good old days." Heavy horses in harness were still a common sight after World War II, until they were finally superseded by tractors. Many breeds were in danger of extinction. Fortunately, they have experienced a renaissance over the last few years. Surprisingly, heavy horse demonstrations and shows have become major attractions throughout Central Europe. Teams of horses pull historic farm machinery and carts; there are weight-pulling competitions and plowing competitions, as well as colorful parades and races. With spectacles such as these, the friendly whoppers are pulling their way from oblivion back into the limelight.

Hobby riders have also discovered the versatility of the delightful "roly-polies." If they are well-trained, they can be used not only in harness, but are equally reliable under all types of saddles and for all riding styles. A team of two stout HP's with nearly two tons live weight can generate up to 50 HP and easily drag off many times their own weight. People are well advised not to smirk at the stolid temperament of draft horses, but rather to admire their serenity and their power. You can trust them with your life.

Holger Bauer was born without fingers but still he is competing successfully at the highest levels. In his spare time, he devotedly cultivates small fields and pastures with his beloved Percherons, moves logs in the forests, shows teams of four or even up to ten horses in parades, and participates in logging and weight-pulling competitions. No distance is too far for him—as long as he finds a heavy horse at his destination! He spent one of his holidays with the Amish People to study their various ways of harnessing and working with their horses.

For Gunther Schopf, an original Bavarian character, the world is centered around horses. It seems almost incredible that—with his amazing horse sense—he has succeeded in navigating his rare and extremely beautiful spotted Noriker horses merely with his voice. This is not only very convenient for photo-shootings, but it is also very impressive if you are driving around Munich in a carriage and the driver never takes up the reins. His greatest pleasure, however, is to harness up four stallions to a Roman chariot in a quadriga and race à la Ben Hur. His motto "win or die" strikes his competitors' hearts with awe. To date—he is still alive!

Photo-shoots with the "heavyweights" are always quite an experience. The huge Percheron stallion Rambo with a canon bone size of nearly 15 inches, by profession a brewery horse, was an overwhelming sight. Yet a nine-year-old girl reaching only up to his chest took him out of his stable without problems. If you see these huge bodies plowing through the snow in winter, you feel the massive power in their movements.

According to the laws of motion, a lot of energy is required to set huge masses in motion. The publisher of my book about heavy horses wanted to witness one of the photo shoots. Of course, he was immediately enlisted to help. Four Schleswig horses dozed in their muddy paddock in the blistering heat and their only response to his desperate attempts to urge them into motion was a tired wiggling of their ears. He looked at me in despair. I advised him to be more energetic. He gave it his all: he jumped up and down, screamed at them, rattled a tin can, and really got on their all-too-good nerves. In slow motion, they started to move their hooves. There was no limit to Hans' ambition. It was impossible to stop his metamorphosis from a serious businessman into a frantic horse scarer. All of a sudden, the geldings broke into a gallop, Hans following them. It was hilarious to watch the four heavy horses splashing through the mud, followed by my publisher, cheering, soaking wet and covered in mud, yet at one with the world. I must admit, I loved his performance!

*Shires are called "Gentle Giants"
because they truly are!*

When I stood vis-à-vis a Shire horse for the first time, I involuntarily held my breath. The gelding was nearly 20 hands and his hooves so enormous that, with my hand on his frog, I could not touch his shoes with my fingertips. To my surprise (and my relief) the frolicking giant knew his stopping distance exactly and was able to jerk to a halt about an inch in front of me. How very considerate of him!

We had neither saddle nor bridle, only an old halter and a lead rope—and a stubble field. Two men clumsily pushed me up into the airy height of about seven feet—whew, made it! And it was quite comfortable, too. The Shire wasn't as stocky as I thought and his brawny flanks formed some sort of "natural saddle." Norcliffe Dylan turned around to look at me wonderingly. I talked to him reassuringly—or rather to myself. Then I nudged him tentatively and the huge animal really set himself in motion. And the way he moved! His size and the length of his strides made my whole body sway. Dylan turned or stopped at discreet twitches on the lead rope. His sensitivity was amazing! Courageously, I asked the black horse to walk a little bit faster. I seemed to absorb Dylan's immense energy and I became daring. *Trot, Dylan!* The gentle giant trudged rhythmically through the field. All my concerns had vanished into thin air; I was carefree. *Come on, Dylan! Let's canter!* Obediently, one ton of horse swung into canter. As if in slow motion, the two of us were flying toward the setting sun. What a wonderful feeling! All too soon we reached the end of the field—no wonder with such a large stride!

On a galloping Shire-back, you feel as comfortable and safe as if you were in a cradle, even without saddle and bridle.

Heavy Horses 65

Jean-François and Frédéric Pignon:

Playing To Success

A small group of horses without halters quietly grazes in the middle of a field. Four gray mares—nice-looking, well groomed, but not very distinctive. With them, a chestnut pony with a blaze—a little bit chubby; also nothing special. The field is located next to a highway and there is no fence. This is strange. A man arrives at the spacious grassland. He utters a short cry. Abruptly, the horses lift their heads from the lush grass and set off in gallop. They don't run away, but head toward the man some 600 feet away from them. The man slightly lifts his arm. Immediately, the horses line up in a perfect row. Next, a nearly invisible cue. The five mares rear up, and then kneel down. He hops onto their croups, and walks over them as if on a pedestrian crossing. The horses don't move a muscle. Unbelievable. Jean-François Pignon makes his horses perform like perfectly trained dogs, yet without restricting them in any way. He presents them in all their power, elegance, and at the same time, in their violability. His liberty act is breathtaking. He is a "horse magician" who enchants and amazes amateurs and experts alike.

The unassuming Frenchman invested years of hard work into this "miracle." Jean-François knows his horses inside and out. He knows their characters, their preferences, their strengths, and their weaknesses. The mares react promptly and reliably to their names. At any moment, no matter where, they are ready to fully concentrate on their two-legged leader. He talks to them, mostly with his body, and this is what the horses understand best. He gives them no treats, but instead a continually quiet and confident manner. He handles them with endless patience, consequence, and fairness. Playful elements, affection, and praise play a vital role in his work. These are the ingredients of Jean-François's phenomenal success—with all types of horses, no matter how old.

After Pignon's breathtaking shows, thousands of people often do not leave, but sit very quietly for a few moments, some even with tears in their eyes. They cannot believe what they have seen.

Usually, Pignon gets his horses from friends or he buys them at regular horse markets. He always hopes to somehow find the right ones. Gazelle was the first one—and exactly the right one. She was a gift to seven-year-old François and his eight-year-old brother Frédéric from their father André, a poor farmer. They got only the horse, no saddle or bridle. Instead of playing football, the two boys played with the mare, just as they do today. Soon the two boys skillfully galloped around bareback, always trying to outdo each other in reckless maneuvers and acrobatic exercises. And they still had neither saddle nor bridle. So they had to control the mare in a different way. The children had no choice; by watching the horse closely, they learned to communicate with the mare in another language—a language that is soft and natural, yet confident and reliable. Ever since, Pignon's horses obey voluntarily and with pleasure. There is no secret, only mutual respect:

"If humans respect horses, they will also respect them as their leaders! The most important prerequisites are inner calmness and balance. Nothing works with force or too much ambition, with punishment or impatience. The whole herd has to consider the human as their leader and guardian, which is only possible if he or she shows superior and considerate behavior. Then the animals will trust their human leader and will do anything just to please him or her!" Your horse spooks easily, is difficult to catch, load, and regulate? Pignon does not have these problems with his horses.

The acts the Frenchman does with his capricious, four-legged ladies Kiowa, Azaria, Aziel, Lais, and Isis can only be described as world class. He calls Azaria, provokes the gray mare, runs around her. She puts her ears flat back and nips at him. It is a put-up job for Pignon. Fully concentrated, he holds a silent dialogue with his horse. Then he swings himself on the horse's back and makes the mare rear. He sits on her backwards, folds his legs around her neck, and bolt upright she rears again. After that, the Frenchman makes the horse lie down, somersaults over the mare, and then turns her on her back. Motionless, Azaria remains in this odd pose.

Lais does caprioles. Just like that. In the middle of the field. Just like in the animated film *Spirit*, she bucks off Jean-François on command and then self-confidently puts her front foot on the chest of her "fallen rider." They do all this without any tack! Passage, piaffe, Spanish walk, sitting, lying down, and rearing! No Problem. Azaria even puts her front hoof on Jean-François' head or gallops alongside Lais with Pignon standing on their croups. All the exercises are carried out calmly, as if by remote control, yet nothing would happen without this man. When we return to the stable, they again pick at some blades of grass peacefully—and alone. Completely unimpressive. Modest stars. As is Jean-François Pignon.

In Avignon, brother Frédéric performs an equally spectacular liberty act with his horses. He, however, prefers to work with stallions. Amidst a pasture covered in flowers Lusitano Fausto kneels down, doesn't look left or right—although another stallion is lying next to him, quietly nibbling at some tufts of grass. A short call and both stallion sit upright in the flowers. Laughing, Frédéric sits down between their front legs and tries in vain to push away Aetes' muzzle which touches his face affectionately: "He always does that! If I don't push him away, he will spend half an hour kissing me and slobbering all over my face."

Just like Jean-François' horses, Frédéric Pignon's show horses are powerful and spirited characters. Even in huge arenas or in the great outdoors, they can be maneuvered and led without any treats individually or synchronously. The stallions are completely free, dance and romp around as if they were only playing and could run away at any moment. Yet, like puppets on invisible strings, they unfailingly return to Frédéric and sweep each audience off their feet with their fantastic performances.

It was hard work for Frédéric to gain the trust of his star Templado, much harder than one would think today. Behind this success is an endless amount of effort, patience, and expertise. The impressive gray stallion is far from being easy to handle. "My parents sold him when he was six months old," Frédéric's wife Magalie tells us. "But he didn't like his home and became more and more anxious. When he was five years old, we felt so sorry for him that we bought him back." Frédéric persevered for two years with the Lusitano with the undulating, long mane. "It was nearly impossible to touch him at all. It was extremely dangerous to enter his stable and when he was out at grass he ran around like crazy—we needed hours to catch him. Riding was out of the question. Nobody can really afford to spend so much time with just one horse. But he taught me to become even more sensitive and, above all, not to count the hours when you are working with horses! Compared to him, any other horse is easy to handle."

Shortly before he leaves for the U.S., Frédéric lets Templado dance for us one more time. We are speechless. As with his brother, we are moved to tears. Apologetically, Frédéric says: "I didn't want to make you cry, I just wanted to give you a special treat!" Thank you! That's what you have done!

Templado is not an easy horse, but Frédéric knows how to handle him. After years of hard work, he can let him run free in almost any location.

Lots of Fun

Photographs depict reality… Or so they say. Horse photos do, for at least one split second. There are, however, humorous photos that make it hard to keep a straight face. On those occasions, you simply can't help but humanize the animals. Some horses just look too funny in certain photos! These "human traits" are, of course, only due to the fact that at the exact moment the shutter is released, the result is perceived in the eye of the human beholder. But seriously, horses have so many wonderful traits. Why shouldn't they make us laugh once in a while?

I know certain horses that have never been trained before who come up with new tricks all by themselves. And they do this, or so it seems, only to please their owners, as they are usually not rewarded with any treats but only with convulsions of laughter! Mares curl their upper lips; noble Iberian horses stick out their tongues; pony Ben balances diligently with his four hooves on some wobbly cavaletti pole, while small, gray Grisou walks on his hind legs and Fjord pony Mondrian enthusiastically pops all the balloons he can get hold of with his teeth. Connemara stallion Sydserff Riverdance, called JJ, catapulted himself, without rider or any inducement at all, from a standstill over a picnic table, at which someone had just settled down to have a nice cup of coffee. We could not believe our eyes when we looked at the photo that we had just taken by chance as a reflex. And the last straw: the little rascal stuck his tongue out at us immediately after his stunt. Honestly, I swear!

Lots of Fun 79

The Maremma:
An Unforgettable Ride

The Maremma: History, the present, nature, and culture melt into a fantastic fresco in these former marshes situated on the shinbone of the Italian "boot." The landscape is a mixture of fragrant pine groves, colorful macchia slopes, ample lagoons, and jagged limestone. There is a long lasting tradition of breeding cattle and horses here. In order to maintain the innate qualities of the Maremmano horse despite the inbreeding of thoroughbred bloodlines, the horses grow up semi-wild in all of the stud farms. Similar to their Americans colleagues, the Italian cowboys (known as *Butteri)* have a deeply ingrained horse sense and even beat Buffalo Bill's troops in a horse breaking competition many years back…

Now the time has come to mount. Maremmano Zorro waits dutifully, his Roman nose and his long ears drooping. Certainly, the dark bay horse is not a beauty, but when his owner rode him I could see his willingness to perform. Powerful move-off, staggering agility: traits that are vital given the huge Maremma cattle with their long curved horns. As soon as I take up the reins Zorro sets himself in motion. First in walk, moving diligently over clay tracks baked into concrete, between razor sharp grasses, rugged pieces of rock, uneven ground, broad crevices, and treacherous quagmires. When I put my leg very softly on the girth, the horse turns as fast as lightning. Oops. Who is asleep here? Obviously, the horse is only pretending to dawdle away sleepily and I was stupid enough to blunder into the trap— foolishness is always in the saddle, not under it! Well-trained Maremmano horses can keep up with any high-performance western horse—perhaps not in terms of looks

but definitely in terms of speed, willingness to perform, and obedience to the rider's aids. If I keep my legs on his body a little bit too long, the dark bay horse starts to do spins. How can he do that on this stony ground? I move my weight out of the saddle and Zorro shoots off. Each slight shift in my weight causes the horse to do flying changes. Thrilled, I forget the disastrous ground and try out ever more rapid movements. Bored, Zorro shakes his long ears. Apparently, he does not consider this appropriately demanding work.

Smirking, my host Lorenzo hands me his working stick, the *uncino*, and points with lively gestures to some long-horned cattle grazing at some distance. Experienced Zorro rounds up the huge cattle almost on his own; I am a mere passenger on his back. Suddenly one of the gigantic bulls breaks away and faces us, his head lowered threateningly and one hoof pawing grimly. I am scared silly, but my Maremmano horse reacts immediately. He ducks down his head and starts to swing from right to left to obstruct the passage out into the open marshes. Alert and with his ears pricked (yes, Zorro can indeed prick his ears if necessary), the horse moves toward the awe-inspiring horned animal. Eventually I work up all my courage to strike out with the uncino and hit the bull crisply on his nose. This is the moment Zorro has been waiting for: he gives a relaxed snort and pushes the one ton animal back into the herd. In the wink of an eye, the unimposing gelding has taught a rookie how to maneuver semi-wild cattle. Like a schoolgirl I fall for my four-legged teacher. He is to be sold for a ridiculous price and I really have to check myself not to buy him on the spot.

Our next task is to find a herd of 30 young stallions. After half an hour they find us: neighing loudly, a dark bay horse breaks through the brushwood. Three-year-old Concerto is a wonderful animal and his thoroughbred sire has left his mark. Lorenzo is not as excited about Concerto's appearance as I am because the youngster soon turns into an insistent admirer of our geldings. The Buttero tries hard to chase him away. Skillfully, the stallion always manages to evade him time and again. The horse's twinkling eyes seem to mock the man. It is interesting for me to watch the two types of the same breed: the rough, old-type Maremmano under the saddle and the modern-type, more elegant youngster. Lorenzo grins: "Go get him!"

With the aid of my sturdy gelding I try to push away the graceful three-year-old. Concerto joins in on the game. It looks as if we are knit together by invisible yarn; in parallel we move through the swamp. The stallion shakes his head with joy; he is enthusiastic about his new "playmate." During the following minutes I experience one of the most stirring rides that I have ever had. My perfectly trained working horse dashes for-

ward at breakneck speed. Concerto has no problem keeping up and is glued alongside us. Together we move in large circles, changing the leads, race on grassland, splash through water, and thunder over concrete-like clay. I could have gone on forever.

Of course, I do not succeed in banishing Concerto and so he persistently keeps us company. I am more than happy about it. Not only do I owe him the fascinating *pas de deux* but, in the end, also one of the best photographs of this trip. While Lorenzo poses in silhouette between tufts of swamp grass, the young stallion approaches him unexpectedly in gallop, stops directly in front of him, stretches his neck, and the two horses touch noses. Lorenzo is as tense as I am—he expects the young stallion to attack his horse viciously any moment while I try different takes and tell him repeatedly not to move on *any* account! Before Concerto becomes too intrusive, I release my Italian friend from his "modeling job." To this day, Lorenzo keeps this photograph on his desk.

Opposite: Concerto is actually a Maremmano-halfblood and was bred from one of the oldest studs in the southern part of Tuscany, "Torre Trappola." For three years, the horses grow up almost wild and very healthy on big pastures in the middle of the Maremma National Park. Then they are used for trailriding, hurdle races, or show jumping.

Page 90: The tack of the Italian cowboys, called Butteri, is very traditional and a mixture between Western and Portuguese saddles.

Pure Joy of Life

Horses simply love running around. They enjoy flexing their muscles, arching their tails in the air, rising up powerfully on their hind legs, and then thundering off at full speed. In between the gallop strides they buck exuberantly and toss their heads joyfully. After repeating their show a couple of times, they pause for a moment to look around with widely flared nostrils, as if to ask: *Has everyone seen us? Aren't we simply fantastic?* We urge them to move again. They react on the spot, hooves flying with delight. The photo shoot is a game for the animals, in which they join all too willingly. Ecstatically, they frolic around me, kicking with all four legs, nipping at each other playfully, and visibly pleased with their elegant bodies bristling with power and strength. In the wilderness, physical health and fitness are a guarantee for survival. This is why horses like to feel that they are in top condition and savor such occasions to the full.

Unrestricted, free movement in full gallop: that is the ideal pay for many four-legged models whose lives—in my opinion—have been too sheltered for too long, or who have simply been forgotten in their box stalls. Looking into their eyes, I know what they long for and ask permission to photograph them. Quite often, I get my best photos with such horses.

Pure Joy of Life 95

96 *Pure Joy of Life*

North Africa:
Diving into Another World

Off we go at a gallop through North Africa, into a dramatic sunset. Behind me is the deep blue sea, beneath me a spirited, compact horse; there is no obstacle in front of me. No roads. No holes in the ground. Only sand. Nothing but undulating sand dunes. What else can you wish for?

When I was twelve years old, I had my first really touching experience with horses during a holiday in North Africa. Near our hotel, there were some camels and horses that served as a tourist attraction, so for the three weeks of our holiday I lived every horse crazy teenage girl's dream! Together with a friend of the same age, I spent the whole day riding the stallions bareback, spoiled them with dry bread and fruit, swam with them in the Mediterranean, galloped among other holidaymakers, jumped over bath towels, and ventured on excursions into the boondocks. Two days before we were to leave for home my favorite stallion colicked and rolled in the sand, groaning with pain. For hours on end, I walked the bay horse on the beach until well after sunset. He felt a lot better the next day and it was time to say good-bye. With a heavy heart I returned to the hotel after having given him his farewell cuddles. At the hotel, I was welcomed by surprised looks. I turned around to find the stallion standing behind me. He had torn off his halter and plodded along, all the way to the hotel. Luckily enough, my parents witnessed the scene. Who would believe such a moving story? Back home, I eagerly set to work to write a twelve-page essay on my holiday adventures. My first article on horses, so to speak, which I was asked to read at school as "my most exciting holiday adventure" (but only because the teacher wasn't aware how much had happened on my holiday!).

I did not return to North Africa until about fifteen years later, yet I have never forgotten this incident. It had a lasting influence on my feelings toward the horses of that part of the world. The genuine North Africa starts where the invasion of streams of tourists ends. In the countryside and especially in the mountains, you often look in vain for the comforts one usually takes for granted, such as electricity, sanitary facilities, and running water. But for all that, or maybe just because of it, the extremely hospitable people have an innate kindness, openness, and contentedness that can hardly be found anywhere in our "civilized" world, and it makes one feel ashamed of one's own pettiness.

While I was collecting information for my book about the legendary horses of the Berbers I visited Jaziret al Maghreb, the "Island of the Setting Sun," as the Arabian conquerors called this vast, 1,900-mile area stretching along the Mediterranean Sea. Until 500 AD, the area which comprises Tunisia, Algeria, and Morocco was mainly populated by tribes we call "Berbers." They call themselves "Imaziren," which means "free people." They were exceptionally gifted riders, and their most valuable possessions were their horses. Later, the Arabs superimposed their culture on the population and the entire region. However, there was one thing that both peoples had in common: their love of horses, borne by overwhelming pride.

Barb horses want to know exactly with whom they are dealing. Good-natured as they may be, one has to earn their respect. Once this is settled, they change their behavior. They are yours for a lifetime and will go through thick and thin with and for their human partner without reservation. "Dogs you can ride" is how this behavior is described in literature.

"Wait and see" perfectly describes the mindset of North African horses (and people!). Most of the time, a thoughtless flight through the inaccessible, jagged mountain region holds more risk than the source of danger one is fleeing from. Therefore, the horses need courage and excellent nerves to survive. If need be, the stallions will even take on a lion. The Barb horses also owe their agility and their power to accelerate to the demanding terrain. Many of them move like cats and they visibly enjoy bounding around like rubber balls!

Above: For this Tunisian Bedouin, his horse means everything: representation, reputation, business, wealth, and tradition.

Opposite: The Arab-Barb is the most common breed in Morocco and combines the elegance of the Arab with the Barb stamina and good temper.

Black stallion Kartoum was to be photographed on the famous "red soil." At six o'clock in the morning we got up, scooped water from the deep well, and washed the horse. At seven o'clock, a pickup van rumbled toward us. Kartoum was to jump onto the loading area nearly three feet above the ground. He refused (which I could absolutely understand). Four men blindfolded him with a garbage bag and somehow hoisted him onto that rickety vehicle. After one hour's drive on bumpy tracks (in this country, nobody could or would do that to their horse) the valuable stallion—in good spirits and neighing loudly—deftly jumped backwards to the ground. Kartoum, carefully watched by my Moroccan companions, was rewarded with two hours of posing for me and frolicking around in a valley near Khenifra. This was a completely new experience for the black stallion, because horses in Morocco are only taken out of their stables when they are ridden or for work. In return, the stallion bestowed me with unique photographs that were more than adequate compensation for the long, exhausting journey.

In Tunisia I worked with Bedouins in the Sahara. I was especially fascinated by the charisma of an old man and how lovingly he handled his horse. Although we did not speak a common language, we understood each other right from the start: the passion for horses pulls down language barriers all around the world. I took many photographs and promised to send them to the address he had scribbled on a piece of paper. When I mailed the photos from home, I was very skeptical as to whether they would ever reach the Bedouin tents. Years later, on Christmas Eve, my phone rang. Someone told me in broken English: "The tribe has asked me to inform you that the old man has died, but your photographs will enshrine his spirit in our tents." My photos had indeed reached their destination!

This page: The warm colored red soil around Khenifra/Morocco created a perfect and typical North African atmosphere for the black Arab-Barb stallion Kartoum.

Page 106: Rider Mimoun rides Arab-Barb Kebir. The stallion looks a lot like a Spanish Andalusian horse—a breed that was created by his ancestors.

Page 107 right: The traditional fantasia-tack is all handmade and very precious. It costs more then a regular year's salary.

Kisbéri Horses and Shagya Arabians:

Hungarian Jewels

On this early morning, the sun fights a futile battle against the heavy rain clouds. Nature wakes with a vengeance, welcoming the life-giving rain after a long drought. Scads of fluffy acacia seeds cover the ground like snow. Somewhere in the steaming wafts of mist tangled between the ancient trees, hundreds of birds greet the refreshing air with their song.

Far away on the horizon, a herd of mares grazes beneath the delicate acacia trees. These horses are not bothered by cold, heat, or rain. Living outside all year, they are inured from an early age to all kinds of weather. Now the mares are nibbling with pleasure at the sweet, white acacia blossoms while their foals lie sleeping in the wet grass. One of them was born the night before, sheltered by the herd, not by a stable. This is also the reason why the herd has moved unusually close to the stud farm. The animals know that they will be helped in an emergency, and they sense that the humans are as interested in the newborn as they are themselves.

The foals, thriving in these conditions, slowly start the day. One after the other, they finally stand up. Then they go and meet their friends, scramble together through the brushwood, snuffle around, and have a good scrub on knotty trees before returning to their mothers for a hearty gulp of milk for breakfast.

We accompany János Lóska on his morning rounds. The well proportioned, shining mares with lots of spirit are all his pride and joy. He gives 25-year-old Szirka an especially long and loving look: the old mare will have her last foal in July. A short whistle and dozens of fine, expressive heads turn toward us. Calmly, the noble horses

set themselves in motion and stroll over to us. Big, friendly eyes gaze at us curiously; some soft muzzles carefully touch our faces. János welcomes each individual mare, strokes each one fondly and appraises each of them with his eyes. Among them, there are many celebrities of the Kisbéri breed; some compete very successfully or win show after show.

In the horse breeding business, success is often based on leaving beaten tracks: having enough courage to ignore the experts' advice and simply do "his own thing." János Lóska did not pay attention to fashion; he searched for and found long lost bloodlines of high quality Hungarian Kisbéri horses, pinned all his hopes on them—and won with flying colors. Today he is the proud owner of the best horses in Hungary.

His elegant, well-muscled stallions frolic around with exuberant vitality and react immediately to even discreet aids, yet at any moment allow you to calmly put on a halter. Excellent character and conformation paired with an irresistible charisma and eagerness to perform in top level jumping and eventing competitions—this combination is extremely rare among warmbloods.

Why is there hardly any information to be found on Kisbéri horses? Why are these horses more or less unknown outside of Hungary? Are there too few riders who appreciate performance and beauty? Too few sensitive riders who can do these animals justice? Or is there a marketing problem? We don't know. Many tourists travel regularly to Hungary and discover this wonderful country while trail riding on the backs of these very special horses. Some of them are unable to resist their qualities and charms and take a Kisbéri home. They then have one of the most exclusive breeds in Europe in their stable.

Kisberis are very rare and almost unknown outside of Hungary (a secret tip if you are looking for a reasonably-priced, compact sport-horse, raised in the very best natural environment).

(Right top and bottom) Janos Loskas excellent and fiery Kisberi-stallions Porthos and Aramis are already successful in Hungarian three day events.

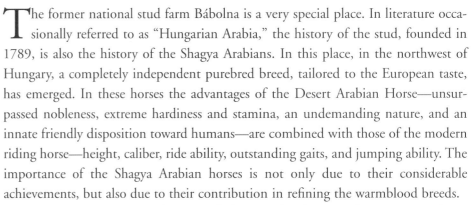

The former national stud farm Bábolna is a very special place. In literature occasionally referred to as "Hungarian Arabia," the history of the stud, founded in 1789, is also the history of the Shagya Arabians. In this place, in the northwest of Hungary, a completely independent purebred breed, tailored to the European taste, has emerged. In these horses the advantages of the Desert Arabian Horse—unsurpassed nobleness, extreme hardiness and stamina, an undemanding nature, and an innate friendly disposition toward humans—are combined with those of the modern riding horse—height, caliber, ride ability, outstanding gaits, and jumping ability. The importance of the Shagya Arabian horses is not only due to their considerable achievements, but also due to their contribution in refining the warmblood breeds.

Since privatization, everything at Bábolna is in shipshape condition: cast iron horse heads on all metal posts; stuccoed ceilings; thick carpets in the long aisles; exquisite glass doors with engraved horse motifs. These days, it is the flag of the European Union that is blowing in the wind in the picturesque inner courtyard with the bronze statue of the legendary stallion Shagya. The fountain is surrounded by flower beds and a chandelier twinkles in the windows of the riding hall, which are made of cut glass. You can have an excellent meal in the adjacent restaurant with its historical ambience, visit the museum, or spend a night in the hotel next to the stables.

At five o'clock in the morning I took my favorite photo in the mares' stable, when the first rays of sunlight peeked in through a window and gently touched a gray mare sleeping on the straw bedding.

The Hungarian Babolna-stud farm is famous for its Shagya-Arabians, a typical Hungarian type of pure bred Arabian, which were the favorite horses of the Austrian-Hungarian cavalry officers.

Magical Details

Often it is just a small detail that makes something very special. I am fascinated by the sounds horses make: a gentle snort, a soft welcoming neigh, or the soothing chewing sound of their teeth. Unfortunately, these sounds can not be captured in a photograph and therefore I turn my attention and my lens to other details. There is a lot to discover. A horse's eyes mirror his soul. Sleepy or relaxed, curious or shy, anxious or excited—they are a reflection of the horse's inner self. Sadly, there are also eyes with a look of resignation, or even eyes that are virtually "dead." Some eyes are wrinkled in sorrow—eyes reflecting the silent agony of a quiet creature. Look closely yourself and ponder about what you see!

Tails blowing in the wind, elegantly pleated manes, quivering ears, inflated nostrils or the silky, freshly washed feathers of Shire horses, Clydesdales, or Irish Cobs are a feast for my eyes. But there are also appealing accessories such as fine leather, artistically forged bits, richly adorned embroidery, neatly polished brass pieces, brocade with fine golden patterns, colorful woolen pompons, exotic braids: each region, each riding style, and each breed has its own characteristic equipment and many a tack room holds real treasures.

In poorer countries, the equipment is often worth more than a year's salary and must last for a lifetime. If you pay close attention to the details, you will realize how amazingly practical some of the solutions really are. The North African ring curb bit may seem brutal to us, but it is only as strong as the hands using it. For the native horses it is a perfectly acceptable bit. And it does have a distinctive advantage: you don't have to worry about losing your curb chain…

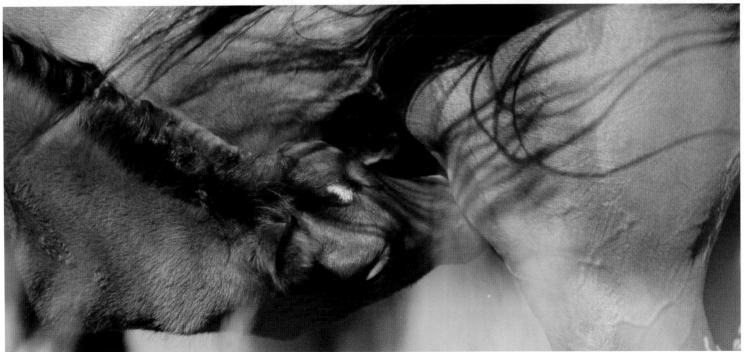

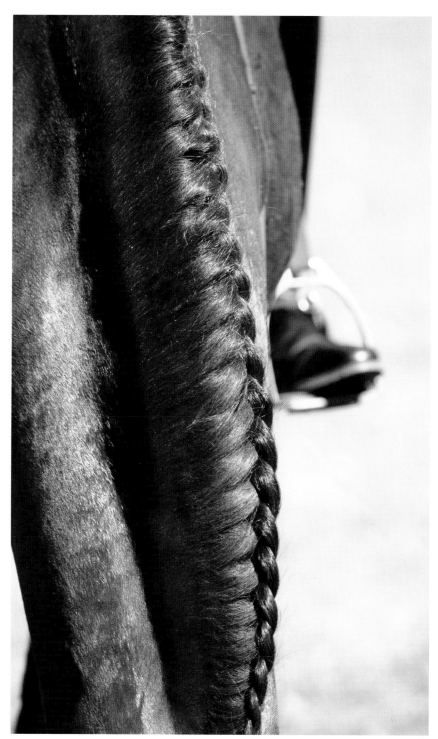

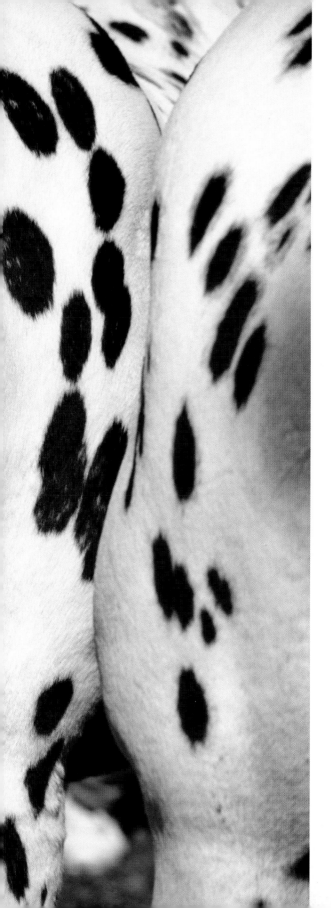

Iceland:

Nature and Adventure

Living off a sparse land, their manes combed by incessant wind, their coats cleansed by numerous showers but lovingly stroked by human hands, the modest Icelandic horses have gained my respect as well as my love with their amiable ways and their unceasing willingness to perform. On the spur of the moment, I decided to join some local breeders and their herds on their four-day ride to Landmannalaugar, some 130 miles away. Before this first visit to the island made of fire and ice, I didn't know a lot about this breed. Now I admire the small yet untiring Icelandic horses just as much as the phenomenal landscape of their home country.

Our adventure starts in the foothills of the mighty Hekla volcano. Clouds of dust, raised by hundreds of vigorous hooves, announce the horses many miles in advance. All of a sudden dozens of horses appear on the horizon. They are rambling about, unconcerned by Hekla's last, sudden eruption only two years ago, unconcerned by the gusty winds that are tearing at our clothes. We are riding at a fast pace and have to change horses regularly, depending on the terrain, in order not to tire them. The next stop is beside a thunderous waterfall. Thankfully the riders sip their steaming hot coffee, bracing themselves with some cookies while their mounts indulge in rolling joyfully in lava sand, nibbling some grass, or turning their rumps protectively against the storm. Thirty minutes later the men select the new mounts. Patiently and calmly they move among the horses who are huddled together protectively. As soon as one of the horses feels eye contact, he tries to disappear. He pushes his way through the other horses, their ears flat back, jerking their heads up, rolling their eyes, baring their teeth to remind the fugitive of his rank within the herd. This game is repeated

quietly until, all of a sudden, the horse is rooted to the spot, as if hypnotized. He accepts the gentle human touch on his body; he allows the hand to pet him even on his head, and accepts the bridle without hesitation. After each break we witness this same amazing spectacle and finally we are convinced that the horses enjoy this mock chase.

Once we reach the plateau, the views become more and more spectacular. Each new mountain we conquer grants us magnificent and ever more surprising vistas of various types of majestic landscape. Steep hills glow in a lush yellow with spots of green and red; sandy plains gleam invitingly in shades of cream and maroon; deep blue lakes abundant with trout reflect the stunning surroundings including our small herd passing by. Spots of sunlight illuminate the hills and create awe-inspiring plays of light. Light and darkness, quietness and storms, black lava and white ice, bizarre moonscapes and bright green carpets of moss—no Hollywood stage director could create such spectacular special effects as does Mother Nature in Iceland! On horseback, we cross swampy grassland, steaming springs, rock massifs overgrown with lichen, rubble plains and dusty fields of lava. Landmannalaugur is part of the Fjallabak Nature Reserve. Strong volcanic activity makes steam leak from the earth all through the valley. It wafts toward the sky in shreds, glistening eerily in the back light. The basic fierceness of this deserted landscape is of such intensity that we sit, deeply moved, on our calmly toelting Icelandic horses.

One week later we organize a photo shoot at the gigantic Skógafoss, the well-known waterfall in the south of the island. There are 80 horses behind our cottage but due to the inclement weather, lighting conditions are bad. Our four-legged models are needed to add splashes of color to the photos. Unfortunately there is only one chestnut with a light mane. I need two. No problem for our host, Julius Aevarsson. "Let's just buy or swap one." This attitude is strange for us but in Iceland this is done all the time. "I have a nice mare, what do you have?" This short conversation is enough and the horses change hands. Just like that: no money involved, no contract, no vet, and no hassle. We quickly find the horse we want in the neighbor's herd, put him on the trailer and off we go. As we drive, giant volcanic rocks massifs covered in glaciers are on our left, marshes to the sea on our right. Then Hawaii and Kauai appear on our left, Holland on our right. This is only possible in Iceland. In our trailer we have four Icelandic horses of various colors, some electric fencing, and feed. A number of tourist buses are sitting in the Skógafoss parking lot. Tourists from all around the world are watching with interest as we unload the horses. Unbelievable as it may seem, if you don't know where to go, you can spend weeks in Iceland without seeing even one horse. The horses follow us obediently to the foot of the waterfall. The view is simply fantastic! Masses of water thunder down 200 feet. We have forgotten the drizzle as the spray from this overwhelming force soaks us to the bone within seconds. The horses are completely unimpressed. The tourists are excited at seeing the horses, and make way for our mobile outdoor studio. The two chestnuts get on really well and immediately begin searching for anything edible in the lava soil. Their color is perfect for the dark background. The tourists behind me seem to agree, as they do the same as me and take as many photos as they can. Just as I begin to wonder what the scene would be like in sunlight, the sky opens for a few seconds to allow the sun to glimpse through the heavy clouds. Rays of sunlight refract in the cloud of spray from the waterfall, creating billions of sparkling water droplets. Only very briefly, but long enough to take a photo, there is a blazing rainbow right behind the two horses. Time seems to stop for an instant. A murmur goes through the crowd. The horses lift their heads in bewilderment—but the miracle has already disappeared. This is Iceland, a country full of variety and surprises!

A symbiosis between humans and horses, climate and landscape, which is so perfect and so well-established as it is on this island made of fire and ice, is hard to find. Even in today's technically advanced age, people in Iceland prefer to rely on the unmistakable instincts of their animals in critical situations rather than on modern methods of navigation. These tough horses can only develop their strengths to their full capacity in their place of origin. Here, they don't suffer from "civilization diseases" and are real partners for their humans. I am already looking forward to my next visit.

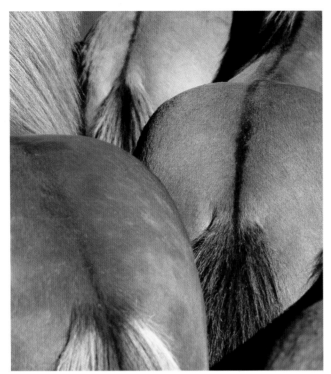

Straight from the Horse's Mouth

Horses are real chatterboxes. They talk all the time: "What's going on over there?" "Oh yes, I like that," "Leave me alone!" or "That hurts!" In order to understand them, we don't need to use our ears so much, but rather our eyes as horses communicate more with their bodies than with their voices. In the wilderness, each sound could call the attention of predators to them and therefore they both enjoy and suffer in silence. Domesticated horses are the exception, especially if they want to contact other horses. Depending on the situation, there are various neighs: the tender, welcoming nicker of a mare, or the authoritative scream of the stud with his teeth bared (of course, he keeps his teeth hidden out of decency when a newcomer neighs a friendly "hello"). With horses, everything works with body language, and so they can't help but communicate!

You can see reluctantly pinched mouths and nostrils or upper lips extended with pleasure, e.g. when rolling. A stallion makes the same passionate face if he catches the sight and smell of a mare in season! Obviously, there are certain parallels in the emotional world of humans and horses. Perhaps this is why an alarming number of riders seriously expect their horses to understand human language. However, the riders themselves know almost nothing about animal language.

The horse's ears are remarkably mobile. They signal into which direction the horse's attention is drawn. Pricked with interest or curiosity, nervously flicking or tiredly laid out laterally and opened to the ground, they give a clear indication of the horse's mood level. Ears pinned back and threateningly bared teeth are understood by just about everyone. I wonder how our horses perceive us in this respect. After all, our ears are pinned back all our lives…

Due to the position of their eyes, a horse's field of view is almost 360 degrees. Horse eyes are among the largest and most expressive in the whole of the animal kingdom and they speak a language all of their own: eyes gazing with interest, eyes wide open with fear, eyes threateningly rolling, eyes blinking tiredly, or eyes dull with resigned suffering. Not only sick animals have such a blank look in their eyes, but also those animals that have to give their peak performance every time. Their eyes are very different to those of a relaxed and happy horse. In a herd, each member knows his exact place within the hierarchy. Small gestures—one look, wiggling the ears, the position of the head and neck, swishing the tail, or curling their nostrils—are usually enough to assert oneself. Even in genuine conflicts, fights with physical contact are only the last resort.

As you can see, horses really "talk" incessantly, yet not all of their fans bother to listen to them—or rather to watch them—carefully! In my job, however, this is one of the most important tools. Understanding a horse's body language enables me to anticipate his behavior so that I can prepare myself, and my camera, for things to come. Thinking and feeling like a horse is the best prerequisite for taking excellent photographs.

Kladruby Horses: Pompous Elegance in Black and White

Roman noses are ungainly, and large horses can only move clumsily. If this is what you think, you will surely change your mind once you have seen a Czech Kladruby horse of the old type in motion, and let the impressive grandeur of such a horse sink in. Personally, I can't get enough of them. Baroque type horses are round, compact, and somehow "frilly" in their movements. So what do the horses of the even more ornate Rococo era look like? They look like the Kladruby horse of the old type. The representative carriage horses of the Royal-Imperial Court of Vienna are another of the "artistic accomplishments" of this era.

The impressive steeds are full of fire and energy and present themselves nobly. At the same time, they are unbelievably good-natured with nerves of steel. Bolting horses in harness were clearly unacceptable for a royal and imperial monarch! In motion, Kladruby horses display a downright majestic presence—be it in free movement, under the saddle, or in harness. Their long, Roman noses are characteristic of the breed and are an explicit breeding goal. In 1989, the Czech government declared the 600 living gray and black Kladruby horses national cultural monuments. Since then, the same rules apply as for irretrievable art treasures: two governmental departments have to give their agreement if one of these horses is to be sold abroad.

The convex Roman nose is absolutely typical for the Kladruber Horse, a breed that was created for pulling Baroque and Rococo emperor's carriages. The greys were used for representation, the blacks only for ecclesiastical occasions and funerals. The horses are a national Czech heritage and cannot be sold from the Kladruby stud farm without two ministers signing the contract. About 800 horses of this very special breed still exist.

In the Kladruby Nad Labem Stud farm, time seems to have passed without leaving a trace. A magical spell seems to have been cast on this place, and the visitors are captivated by it. For centuries, the mares have left their spacious stables every morning at the same time, in all types of weather. Trustingly, they follow their groom along the long, ancient parkways to the pastures. Every year about 100 foals, born in the protective herd, manage to grow into their too large heads. Little by little, the ugly ducklings bloom into beautiful, elegant swans. Young stallions learn to go in harness by drawing muck and feed carts, thus accommodating the day-to-day needs of the stud farm. Later in their life, they will float with dignity in teams of four across the yard or through the shady woods of the surrounding countryside. The only new encounter is perhaps being under the saddle, yet most of the Kladruby horses master this procedure with royal and imperial composure, belying all skeptics.

On a bitterly cold February night, mare number 255 Afrika gives birth to her first foal. Together, humans and horses witness the miracle of birth in the big, open stable. Deeply stirred, we watch the herd welcome the newcomer; we follow the foal's first attempts to get up on his far too long, shaky legs and see how he enjoys his first drink of milk. The circle of life has started another turn—in Kladruby Nad Labem, hopefully, for many more years to come.

Friends Stick Together

Horses are extremely sociable creatures who feel unhappy without their colleagues around. Despite cases of instantaneous sympathy and antipathy, horses only feel protected and secure in their herd. True buddies like to stick together in every situation, develop synchronized movement patterns, have extensive physical contact as well as very frequent mutual grooming routines, and really seem to suffer if they are separated. A horse alone cannot be a happy horse. He needs the company of at least one fellow of the same species around him, and I am not referring to donkeys, sheep, or goats. And with regard to human company: don't fool yourself. You are not a horse! All the treats in the world and, least of all, new saddle pads or other accessories will not turn you into a horse in the eyes of your horse. So please allow him to share his life with horsey friends!

Csikósi:

Artisans on Horseback

An ocean of green waves moves softly in the wind. Zuza and Alkony, two Nonius mares, trot along briskly and our gig rattles on the dry, deeply furrowed track. We are tossed about, but our driver, greasy hat pulled into his weather-beaten face, is perched relaxedly on the coach box. Everyday life in Hungary. We are on our way to the big herds of Nonius horses in the Hortobágy puszta. Somewhere out there in the great wide open there are gray cattle, racka sheep with bizarre spiral horns, mangalica pigs with comical wool coats, donkeys, water buffaloes and, of course, Hungarian Nonius horses!

Generations of highly esteemed herders have been looking after the various types of animals since the beginning of time. The Csikós, or horsemen, are at the top of the hierarchy. Their deftness on horseback is legendary—especially bearing in mind that not only do they master the "Hungarian Post," but ride with only a piece of leather that has stirrups attached to it but no girth, or else bareback!

This lightweight, handmade "saddle" is called "Prics" and is only used in this area. I am skeptical, but Csikós Bordas Janos thinks that it is really practical: "If I am working out with the herds, I can't keep my horses saddled all day. Besides, if there is an emergency, I can saddle my horse faster without the girth and if I fall, there is no risk of getting caught in the stirrups!" Seems to make sense, but the rest of the riding world doesn't seem to agree….

Standing on galloping horses while driving another pair in front was first shown in a fantasy-painting by the artist Mr. Koch. Some fearless Csikós, the famous horse-keepers of the Puszta, were crazy enough to realize this idea and created the international show-number "Hungarian Post."

I am wondering how to mount when Janos unravels the mystery: one hand reaches over the horse's back and pushes the stirrup leather on the opposite side down, and then the left foot goes into the stirrup iron in front of the horse's elbow and the rider vaults quickly onto the horse. Surprisingly enough, it works—at least when the Csikós do it. Another way to mount is to make the horse lie down, get on the horse's back and have the horse lift you up. This is a trick all of the Csikós' horses know. It is also convenient. Lying horses are used as a wind shelter when the riders want to take a little nap. Both horse and rider virtually vanish from sight in an instant if danger is imminent. Or the Csikós loll comfortably against their sitting horses and smoke their pipes. Today they perform their tricks mainly for fascinated tourists, but all of these stunts have a traditional background.

Hairy Tales

A good horse has no specific color, but a beautiful horse certainly has plenty of long hair. Not only in terms of photography are copious, well-groomed manes and tails—silky fine or heavy curls—by far the most attractive adornment of our beloved steeds. The owners of horses with such "hairy jewels" spare no time or effort in grooming them—and it takes a long time to braid in a tail toupee. Most of the time, it is by pure chance that you succeed in expertly capturing blowing manes on a photograph. Some days just seem to be "bad hair days." Flying manes and tails look their best in the most disadvantageous phases of a gallop. On top of that, the long wisps have a tendency to wrap around the neck like a scarf. So you stop the horse, redo the mane, and before you have a chance to let him run free again, another breeze ruffles the carefully laid tresses anew. The whole photo shoot might even end in disaster if the horse drops his head to take a bite of lush grass, accidentally steps on his undulating luxuriant mane and tears out large tufts of it. On one occasion, a well-known four-legged model pulled out huge pieces of his freshly unbraided and styled, nearly four-foot-long mane—out of pure boredom. We had left him unattended in the aisle for only three minutes and nearly fainted when we saw his (formerly) glorious mane lying at his hooves…

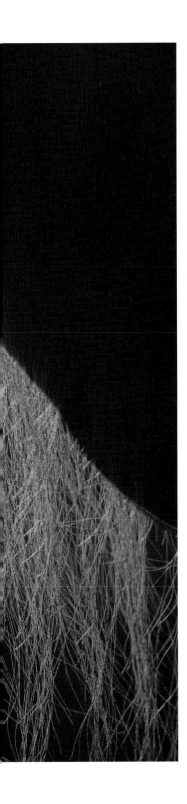

Natural Settings

An amazing aspect of equine photography is its timelessness. I can rejoice in a good photo for many years—even if a colleague took it! Over the years, a photographer naturally develops a certain routine for standard photo series portraying a certain breed, standing photos, and riding poses, but in all my photo shoots I make sure that each horse is portrayed in at least one individual and special motif. Nature assists me with her sheer infinite diversity of moods, colors, and shapes: vegetation and landscapes, water and rocks, shadow and light. For each coat color and each breed there is a setting that perfectly fits one particular horse.

A good photographer has to have the skill of perceiving such extraordinary places, moods, or situations and use them for the photo design. Motifs of "naked" horses amidst natural, picturesque surroundings are especially appealing, but such compositions can sometimes be more than difficult in densely populated Europe. Buildings, streets or, at least, ugly electric fences are everywhere. Letting horses run free without fencing is more or less impossible given the dense traffic. If one doesn't want to spend most of one's time working with PhotoShop on the computer (I abhor this and would rather spend my time with the horses), a lot of experience and a big bag of tricks are required in order to conjure up the vision of a wild and free horse's life—if only in a photograph. A convincing result is all the more fun.

At times, one virtually stumbles across a stunning location. In those cases, a horse that is fitting to the location is selected and driven there. (I would like to use this opportunity to thank the many horse owners who have supported me with their ded-

ication!) Some horses look their best with a certain flower color—and if one is lucky, it can be found close-by. But maybe the flowers will need to be planted and one has to wait patiently until the following year or, alternatively, appropriate flower tubs can be borrowed in a market garden. (Clearly, equine photography is hard work…) However, a good photograph justifies all the efforts—as long as animals and humans remain unharmed. Almost always, at least the humans involved work up a good sweat.

On a hot summer day, six people tried everything for two hours to persuade two young Fjord pony stallions to go into a pond situated in an enchanting location; all efforts were in vain. Resignedly, we swapped the two youngsters for mare Jasmin. She trudged into the pond without hesitation and posed brilliantly for the photos, but then decided not to come out! Some branches dangled within her reach and she happily munched the welcome snack. Thoroughly content with her pool and her snack bar she ignored all our endeavors. In the end, the only thing we could do was to get into the pond and shoo "madame" back to dry land in a splashy chase.

Every once in a while you strike it really lucky. During a storm an impressive but rotting tree had fallen onto the vast field of an Akhal-Teke stud farm. For several weeks, the horses nibbled devotedly at the old giant until only bare, light wood was left over. It was an unexpected, yet wonderfully bizarre setting for the exotic athletes from Turkmenistan.

There was also this marvelous embankment dissecting an Austrian fish pond. We only had to put up two electric fences to allow valuable Lusitanos to run free safely. Tufts of grass and soft back light emphasized the illusion of an idyllic horse heaven—even though its dimensions were only 10x260 feet.

The snow-covered conifer in a friend's garden was smaller still. It stood right between the clothes line and the garden shed. When I saw the tree, my only thought was how to get Knabstrup horse Pike there. With an effort, we managed to maneuver the strikingly spotted, three-year-old horse into the tiny garden and precisely next to the tree so that his quarters were not hidden behind the clothes line. The greedy black and white gelding was served a generous helping of oats directly at the tree trunk and he melted into the green and white background. It took a long time until I had wrenched myself in a position that excluded *all* artifacts of human civilization from the photo and the horse had adopted a natural stance. I cherish this unusual photograph still today.

Ponies:

Small but Powerful

If you enter the world of ponies you have to be on your guard. They don't care at all about their size—or rather the lack of it. Ponies are extremely self-confident, react completely different than horses, and are always game for a laugh! In a big herd, it is usually the smallest ponies that are the leaders. This is also true on Sabine Ellinger's farm. Here is the kingdom of his highness Lancelot, a miniature Appaloosa pony with delusions of grandeur. Originally, he was bought as a companion for a dressage horse, yet the little rascal soon became bored and now he works as a show pony. Finally, he is paid the tribute he thinks he deserves! He definitely enjoys posing for me, as there are always some enticing little mares involved. It is not that he actually needs them to present himself at his best, but a stallion also has to have some fun at a photo shoot…

When I visited the stud farm, 17-year-old German Classic Pony mare Arabella vom Taubergrund, about 9 hands "small," was not even scheduled to be photographed, but her foal was. (The twelfth in a series!) So we took mare and foal to a lovely pasture bursting with wild flowers to allow the little one to scamper around. Arabella waited patiently. In the afternoon, the sky clouded over—end of the photo shoot. I went to the pasture to say goodbye to the sweet ponies.

As soon as I lay on the ground, the ponies approached me nosily. Charming little heads examined me with interest; tiny nostrils blew their warm breath into my face. This was one of those moments when I cherish my job the most, and which can't last long enough. Thomas, my husband, is a wonderful companion and very patient, but once in a while even he gets fed up. He knows that in moments such as these I am lost in reverie. So he pushed me to get going, hinting at the bad lighting conditions. Slowly, I rolled away from the ponies so as not to startle them. "Just *one* more photo as a souvenir," I sighed. No matter if it doesn't turn out. Arabella was finally in a good pose for me to take a portrait. All of a sudden, a fly buzzed along. To this fly I owe one of my favorite photos. The fly crawled into the lovely little mare's ear and made her shake her head just as I pressed the release. The thick, white forelock bounced in perfect curls. A touch of light flickered on her light bay coat. The photo couldn't have been more perfect. This photograph wonderfully sums up this delightful, delicate creature. What a fluke!

Iberian Horses:
Royal Horses – Horse Royalty

Feria de Jerez: The stallion rears playfully, prances and snorts amidst the crowd. His silky mane flows around his arched neck in long strands. His eleven-year-old "caballero" puts on an inscrutable face and casts a cool look over the "infantry," enjoying their admiration. If you visit a "feria" in the South of Spain, it should be on horseback!

Every year in the second week of May, horse lovers from all over the world meet in Jerez. Exhibition halls and sales stalls, innumerable visitors from near and far, parading riders with "*chicas a la crupa*" (women in ornate dresses sitting on the horses' croups), Spanish temperament, flamenco music, sherry, and the famous national dishes "tapas" and "paella"—the atmosphere is intoxicating and unforgettable. For eight days and nights, the young and the old, the Spanish and the tourists all celebrate horses beneath the glistening Andalusian sun. Everyday life comes to a standstill. During that week, everyone is in "feria" fever—and not only in Jerez.

We are tired from walking around all day, but all of a sudden thousands of colored light bulbs illuminate the scene, competing against the velvety blue, starry sky. Who could think of going to sleep at this moment? Who would be foolish enough to go home now? We are swept away into the night, listening to the sounds of the castanets, savoring sherry and tapas. We all agree: without a doubt we want to see them again, the magnificent horses and carriages and the noble riders of Spain!

Below: In Spain, many breeders have little bullfighting arenas, like roundpens. Often, this is the only place where stallions can be shown in freedom. Of course, the spirited horses use the occasion to gallop around and lose a little bit of energy.

Opposite: If a horse is really sensible and highly trained, like this Lusitano stallion Apache, you can work him on "long reins," giving up your legs and weight to get in contact with the animal. Only reins, body position, and voice will tell the horse how to dance in Dressage-Lections.

They are breathtaking: the Spanish horses, officially called "Pura Raza Española" or commonly called Andalusians. Impossible to find a more eye-catching breed! If you are not exclusively interested in show-jumping, no other breed is more apt to leave a permanent impression with spectators (and photographers). In the Baroque era, the European nobility rode on these horses—if they could afford them, as they were worth their weight in gold. The reasons? Pompous exterior, friendly yet fiery temperament, spectacular movements, courage, excellent nerves, striking agility, high intelligence, and a talent for airs of the "haute école." This was and is more than can be expected from a normal horse. Andalusians and their cousins, the Portuguese Lusitanos, were and still are first choice if horse and rider want to put themselves in the limelight.

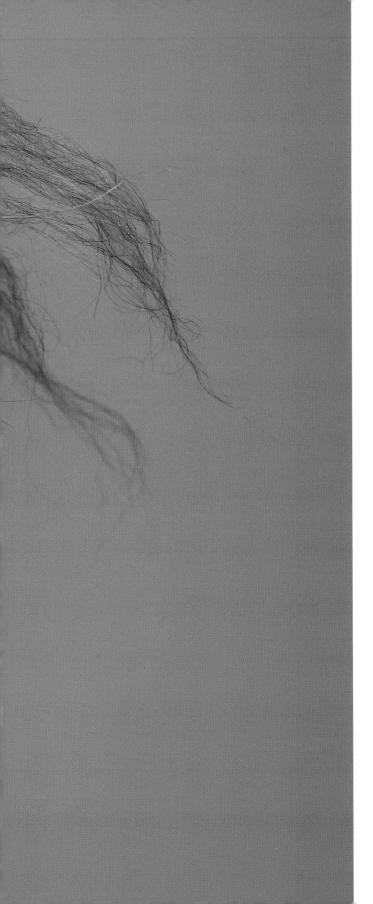

By now, you can tell: I am hopelessly addicted to these wonderful animals. I can't wait for the next photo shoot. For days on end, I could go into raptures about horses and write innumerable pages about them. But as a picture says more than a thousand words, I will let the photos speak for themselves.

Christiane Slawik:
Photo Journalism with Passion

Christiane Slawik has dedicated her life to equine photography. She has been fascinated by horses since childhood and put herself through university by painting and photographing horses. The title of her thesis was: "Hippological Considerations Relating to Naturalistic Horse Portrayals in the Visual Arts." For more than 30 years she has been at home in all types of saddle.

After several visits to the USA, she worked for a radio station and then moved on to a job as an anchorwoman, and was temporary editor-in-chief, for a German television station in which she worked for several years.

Today she writes and photographs for numerous international horse magazines and publishing houses. In search of expressive moments, the photojournalist takes her inspiration from each situation, light and color, the aesthetics and the individual charisma of the horse. Her photographs and her paintings have been exhibited repeatedly.

A Passion for Horses

"No matter whether they are chubby or skinny, big or small, old or young, noble or coarse—I have always been delighted by horses. They attract me magically; they make me shiver with pleasure. Their presence, their facial expressions, their smell and, above all, the sounds they make: a gentle snort, a soft welcoming nicker, or the soothing chewing sound of their teeth…"

Christiane Slawik's 35 years of riding experience started in a conventional riding club with the standard program: lessons, riding holidays, riding qualification exams, and small competitions. She put herself through college (geography, arts and German) by painting horses. Her paintings have been presented repeatedly in exhibitions. With her standard photographic equipment (also used for travel photographs and term papers), she was able to create impressive equine portraits. During extended visits to the U.S., she also used the horses she was riding as models, e.g. Quarter Horses or Saddlebreds. In her thesis she had the opportunity to combine her love of art with her love of horses: her professor recommended widening the scope of her thesis into a dissertation. In her arts exam, both her paintings as well her sculptures portrayed horses.

That Certain Something

At some point, Christiane was able to combine her former hobbies—horses, photography, traveling, meeting animal enthusiasts, and creative work—into a profession, which, for her, is a true vocation with only one restriction: brush and easel have been retired and the "painting" is done solely by the camera. In addition to the popular motifs requested by publishers and customers, Christiane Slawik—as opposed to many of her colleagues—offers her clients and audiences "that special something."

Slawik's photographs clearly demonstrate her background and talent in the arts. They uniquely capture the temperament, charm, and character of each individual animal. One customer enthusiastically said: "You haven't portrayed my horse as everybody sees him, but how I see him in my heart!"

The artist does not only produce "dream photographs," but also initiates new dreams with them: "A really good photograph manifests within a split second everything that we imagine about horses: manes and tails blowing in the wind, twinkling eyes, thundering hooves, gracefulness and power. It conjures up the same emotions in horsey and non-horsey people alike whenever they encounter these wonderful animals."

However, Christiane Slawik doesn't only visit "photogenic" or prominent four-legged stars. She also enjoys launching "completely normal" horses, cuddly ponies, or huge draft horses from the "stable next door" onto the front pages, posters, or calendars of international publications each month.

Well-Founded Photojournalism

Today the photojournalist writes and/or photographs for more than 40 international associations, companies, and publishers. Her clients encompass not only book, but also calendar and magazine publishers. Her own, richly illustrated books, published by Cadmos, are characterized by expert knowledge and carefully chosen photographs. Prof. Dr. Zeeb, one of the most renowned European horse behavioral scientists, wrote the following comment about her book on heavy horses: "The older you get, the more you realize how little you really know. You filled that book with a wealth of expert knowledge and amazing photos! It was a pleasure for me to polish up and complete my knowledge."

The one-time TV editor-in-chief gained journalistic experience directly after college while building up one of the largest private, regional television stations in Germany. Christiane Slawik did features and films covering numerous topics, both domestic and international. She presented innumerable travel and magazine programs for many years. The long list of guests on her colorful live talk shows includes celebrities of all shades: star and starlets, Olympic and world champions, rock and pop stars, Pulitzer and Nobel Prize winners, as well as Federal Ministers and national German leaders. She did not have much spare time for animals then. After a film shooting at a stable and a serious accident in Africa that put all activities on hold for almost eight months, she again focused wholeheartedly on her long standing passion: "Now I will do what I enjoy with all my heart!"

Thorough investigation combined with a keen interest in events, background information, and personalities led to a large number of vivid documentaries and features centered on topics around horses throughout the world. The authenticity of her protagonists is a key criterion for the German photojournalist: "Besides portraying breeds and stud farms, I enjoy stories about true horse-people the most. And they are everywhere. If you keep an open mind and heart, they are suddenly right in front of you: sensitive, fine people who look after their animals extremely well and lovingly, always trying to care for them in the best way possible. Employees with low salaries or retirees make up for their lack of money with dedication, ingenuity and, above all, time. Many a professional rider could learn a lot from these horse enthusiasts."

Her extensive expert knowledge helps Christiane Slawik trace, write and photograph these special stories. No matter what riding style, country, or breed, she spots immediately if the horsemanship is good. Deftly, she calms the riders' nerves, sometimes corrects them a bit and puts them in the right perspective at the right moment. Her dedicated, critical eye is unerring. She appraises the horse more tolerantly than she does their riders and conceals minor flaws by using special perspectives: "Horses are such marvelous creatures: infinitely patient, always honest and open-minded. They

give us their unconditional trust, all their power; they make our souls happy. No species in the entire animal kingdom can compare with horses. Where would humankind be without them?"

At Home in All Types of Saddles

Christiane Slawik's comprehensive know-how is not a coincidence. She makes a point to experience for herself all riding styles and breeds in the natural environment so as to understand which idea and purpose is behind breeds, riders' aids, varieties of saddles and bits: "I am only able to develop a deep understanding of each riding culture if I ride the horses myself in their place of origin." Language barriers become irrelevant, even in the remotest locations as soon as the self-confident men in the saddle realize that the woman photographer is not only enthusiastic about horses, but is even able to ride them. "It is always fascinating to experience how the love of horses tears down language and culture barriers all around the world."

During her travels, she toelts over fields of lava on Icelandic horses, visits horse markets in Ireland, or rides Irish Hunters over cross-country courses, walks among the big herds of national stud farms, tries out the power of Portuguese bullfighting horses, rides spectacular passages on Spanish P.R.E. horses, has no problem staying astride rearing Friesian horses, does sliding stops with

Quarter Horses, rides Arabian champions in Egypt, herds semi-wild bulls with the Butteri of the Maremma, sports with a Camargue stallion in the Rhône Delta, lets Knabstrup horses dance at the royal court of the Queen of Denmark in Copenhagen, does not hesitate to vault onto bareback Nonius horses of the Hungarian Csikós, or gallops through Sahara sand with Bedouins in Tunisia.

Riding Florian Müller's sensitive, exceptional stallion Almanzor several times a week for more than a year during his training was an especially enriching experience for her. Today, the grey is one the most successful and well known show horses in Germany, and it was this spirited P.R.E. stallion that infused her with the special love she has for Iberian horses.

As often as possible she watches the work of Europe's top classical riding masters of our age in order to train her eyes in the absolute perfection and harmony so as to be able to transfer this feeling to other motifs. Extraordinary photo shoots in the parks of historical castles and palaces allow her to capture unique moments between horse and rider in stately settings and thus to revive baroque engravings or paintings—a particular specialty of Christiane Slawik. Just like the photographer, the riders also spare no effort to prepare for a photo shoot as they know that it is worth it!